To: *Neal*

From: *Juanita*

Date: *Nov. 2000*

FOR YOU

A PLACE
CALLED
HEAVEN

Compiled by Catherine L. Davis

Chariot VICTOR
◆ PUBLISHING ◆
A DIVISION OF COOK COMMUNICATIONS

Victor Books is an imprint of ChariotVictor Publishing
a division of Cook Communications, Colorado Springs, Colorado 80918
Cook Communications, Paris, Ontario
Kingsway Communications. Eastbourne, England

A PLACE CALLED HEAVEN
Copyright © 1997 by Victor Books

ISBN: 1-56476-692-6

Original Cover Artwork © Kathy Jakobsen, Licensed by
Wild Apple Licensing.

Editor: Barb Williams

Art Director: Bill Gray

Designer: Big Cat Studios, Inc.

Printed in Canada. All rights reserved.
1 2 3 4 5 6 7 8 9 10 Printing/Year 01 00 99 98 97

INTRODUCTION

What will heaven be like? Prophets and disciples, limited by their experience and knowledge, have tried to describe it. Those of us who have placed our future in God's hands through faith in Jesus Christ know that heaven will be more wonderful than we could ever imagine. And, with grateful expectancy, we count on—cling to—the promise of a place where we will be forever with the Lord.

HEAVEN
A place we can really call "home."

"Now we know that if the earthly tent we live in is destroyed,
we have a building from God, an eternal house in heaven, not
built by human hands.... We live live by faith, not by sight.
We are confident, I say, and would prefer to be away
from the body and at home with the Lord."

2 CORINTHIANS 5:1, 7-8

What will heaven be like,
whether I go there as a result of this
operation (a remote possibility),
or go there later (a certainty)?

Heaven will be my eternal
home with Christ. I'll just move
into the part of his Father's
house he prepared for me. No fixing
up that home, no parts unfinished,
no disappointments on moving day.

No, he's prepared it, he's made it
completely ready, completely
perfect, completely mine.

Joseph Bayly

Faith is the Christian's foundation, hope is his anchor, death is his harbor, Christ is his pilot, and heaven is his country.

Jeremy Taylor

Rejoice in glorious hope!
Our Lord, the Judge, shall come,
And take His servants up to their eternal home.
Lift up your heart, lift up your voice!
Rejoice, again I say, rejoice!

Charles Wesley

When we were saved, the world ceased to be our home. We now have "our citizenship . . . in heaven." (Philippians 3:20)

The Greek word translated "citizenship" is used only in this verse and refers to a colony of foreigners. That certainly is true of Christians. We are the citizens of a foreign place to this world—heaven.

John MacArthur, Jr.

We know only too well that one of those things which changes is our body. We grow old. We develop wrinkles. Our eyesight dims, our stride shortens, our back bends. One day the body, "our earthly tent," will be destroyed.

The seen is temporary, changeable. How wonderful to be able to look beyond our own decaying frames, and know that "we have a building from God, an eternal house in heaven."

Larry Richards

I do not know how long 'twill be,
Nor what the future holds for me,
But this I know if Jesus leads me,
    I shall get home some day.

Charles A. Tindley

My father used to say to us, when we were children and had to go away from home for a while, "Children, don't forget, when Jesus takes your hand, then He holds you tight. And when Jesus keeps you tight, He guides you through life. And when Jesus guides you through life, one day He brings you safely home."

Corrie ten Boom

What's a home like,
one that he prepares?

A place of peace and beauty,
of joy and glory, of celestial music,
of fresh, unchanging, purest love.

I'll say, "Hello, Lord. I'm tired."
And he'll say, "Rest,
because I have
work for you to do."

Joseph Bayly

From years before, I remembered an old song we used to sing in "rounds." One side of the church would sing, "I'm on the homeward trail . . . I'm on the homeward trail . . ." and the other side would come back with "Singing, singing, everybody singing, HOMEWARD BOUND!" . . . Through faith in Christ, we are all homeward bound. As God gradually transfers our loved ones to heaven, we have more and more deposits there, and as 1 Corinthians 2:9 says, "Eye has not seen, nor ear heard, nor have entered into the heart of man the things which God has prepared for those who love Him" (NKJV). What bright hope is in those words. And if ever there were a time we needed hope, it is NOW! . . . IN OUR FATHER'S HOUSE ARE MANY MANSIONS. I HOPE YOURS IS NEXT TO MINE!

Barbara Johnson

My Jesus as Thou wilt.
All shall be well for me;
Each changing future scene
I gladly trust with Thee.
Straight to my home above,
I travel calmly on,
And sing in life or death,
"My Lord, Thy will be done."

Benjamin Schmolck

Goodness and mercy all my life
Shall surely follow me;
And in God's house for evermore
My dwelling place shall be.

Scottish Psalter

My mother used to say that she didn't find any particular attraction in golden streets. I had no answer for her until I read a comment by F.B. Meyer, that in heaven all earth's values are turned upside down. "What do we count most valuable on earth?" he asked. "Gold. Men live for gold, kill for it. But in heaven gold is so plentiful that they pave the streets with it instead of macadam."

Joseph Bayly

For the Lord our God shall come,
And shall take His harvest home;
From His field shall in that day
All offenses purge away;
Give His angels charge at last
In the fire the tares to cast,
But the fruitful ears to store
In His garner evermore.

Even so, Lord, quickly come
To Thy final harvest home;
Gather Thou Thy people in,
Free from sorrow, free from sin;
There forever purified,
In Thy presence to abide.
Come, with all thine angels come;
Raise the glorious harvest home.

Henry Alford

HEAVEN
A place where we'll finally see Jesus,
the Son, and God, the Father.

*"But Stephen, full of the Holy Spirit, looked up to heaven and
saw the glory of God, and Jesus standing at the right hand of
God. 'Look,' he said, 'I see heaven open and the Son of Man
standing at the right hand of God.'"*

ACTS 7:55-56

The blind hymnwriter Fanny Crosby lived life in hope and not in bitterness, and wrote more than 6,000 gospel songs. One of these songs she had not shared with anyone until one day at a Bible conference in Northfield, Massachusetts, Miss Crosby was asked by D.L. Moody to give her personal testimony. At first she hesitated, then quietly rose and said, "There is one hymn that I have written which has never been published. I call it my soul's poem. Sometimes when I am troubled, I repeat it to myself, for it brings comfort to my heart." She then recited while many wept, "Someday the silver cord will break, and I no more as now shall sing; but oh, the joy when I shall wake within the palace of the King! And I shall see Him face to face, and tell the story—saved by grace!"

Kenneth Osbeck

God speaks to us from heaven when we pray. Sometimes the answers are clear; sometimes they are vague; sometimes they say "wait." However, we know that someday we will be with Him in His home, and communications will be crystal clear, because we will be with Him. "Now we see but a poor reflection; then we shall see face to face. Now I know in part; then I shall know fully, even as I am fully known" (1 Corinthians 13:12).

Billy Graham

We are afraid that Heaven is a bribe, and that if we make it our goal we shall no longer be disinterested. It is not so. Heaven offers nothing that a mercenary soul can desire. It is safe to tell the pure in heart that they shall see God, for only the pure in heart want to.

C.S. Lewis

Heaven! It is called the paradise of God—a paradise, to show how quiet, harmless, sweet, and beautiful heaven shall be to them that possess it. . . . These visions, that the saved in heaven shall have of the love of Christ, will far transcend our utmost knowledge here; even as far as the light of the sun at noon goes beyond the light of a blinking candle at midnight.

John Bunyan

Ezekiel concludes his record of remarkable visions with that of the city of God. It is a city of perfect architectural proportions, symmetrical design, free access, and has a healing and life-giving stream. But its crowning glory will be the presence of God in its midst. The final and culminating words of this magnificent book is the name of the city, which interpreted is, *The Lord is There*.

Henry Gariepy

For me the heavenly Bridegroom waits
To make me pure of sin.
The Sabbaths of Eternity,
One Sabbath deep and wide—
A light upon the shining sea—
The Bridegroom with His bride!

Alfred Lord Tennyson

This isn't death—it's glory!
It is not dark—it's light!
It isn't stumbling, groping,
Or even faith—it's sight!
This isn't grief—it's having
My last tear wiped away;
It's sunrise—it's the morning
Of my eternal day!

This isn't even praying—
It's speaking face to face;
Listening and glimpsing
The wonders of His grace.
This is the end of pleading
For strength to bear my pain;
Not even pain's dark memory
Will ever live again.

How did I bear the earth-life
Before I knew this rapture
Of meeting face to face
The One who sought me, saved me,
And kept me by His grace!

Martha Snell Nicholson

Face-to-face with Christ my Savior,
Face-to-face—what will it be—
When with rapture I behold Him,
Jesus Christ who died for me?

Face-to-face I shall behold Him,
Far beyond the starry sky;
Face-to-face in all His glory,
I shall see Him by and by!

Carrie E. Beck

Then shall our will and affections be ever in a burning flame of love to God and his Son Jesus Christ. Our love here hath ups and downs; but there it shall be always perfect with that perfection which is not possible in this world to be enjoyed.

John Bunyan

Soon, from us, the light of day
Shall forever pass away;
Then, from sin and sorrow free,
Take us, Lord, to dwell with thee.

George Washington Doane

Jesus, the very thought of Thee
        With sweetness fills my breast;
But sweeter far Thy face to see
        And in Thy presence rest.

Latin 12th Century

Sunset and evening star,
        And one clear call for me!
And may there be no moaning of the bar,
        When I put out to sea.
For tho' from out our bourne of time and place
        The flood may bear me far,
I hope to see my Pilot face to face
        When I have cross'd the bar.

Alfred Lord Tennyson

What began with the harmless question of a little boy, "Can Martina see us now?" became a never-ending pondering of the whole family on life after death. . . . Many times we have found out that we cannot love what we do not know. We shall know God as He is. Therefore, we shall love Him to an extent inconceivable to us now. We shall be at rest. We shall be happy . . . what will be in store for us when we shall see Him in His risen glory, the fairest of men, the best of friends, the most humble of all masters, He the changeless one!

Maria von Trapp

Still, still with Thee,
When purple morning breaketh,
When the bird waketh,
And the shadows flee;
Fairer than morning,
lovelier than the daylight,
Dawns the sweet consciousness,
I am with Thee.

So shall it be
at last,
in that bright morning
When the soul waketh,
and life's shadows flee;
Oh, in that hour,
fairer than day–light dawning,
Shall rise the glorious thought—
I am with Thee.

Harriet Beecher Stowe

The afterlife is a real place, but most importantly, *heaven is where God is*—where he's with us and we're with him. The ordinary things we value so much in this life are lost in the extraordinary blessing of God's immediate and eternal presence. . . . Heaven is personal, conscious, perpetual, and purposeful existence in the presence of God. We will recognize and enjoy family and friends as well.

Gary Kinnaman

Softly and tenderly Jesus is calling,
Calling for you and for me;
See, on the portals He's waiting and watching,
Watching for you and for me.
Come Home, come Home,
Ye who are weary, come Home;
Earnestly, tenderly, Jesus is calling,
Calling, O sinner, come Home!

Will L. Thompson

HEAVEN

A place where we'll reunite with our
loved ones in joy, worship, and rest.

*"For we know that he who raised the Lord Jesus
to life will with Jesus raise us too, and bring us
to his presence, and you with us."*

2 CORINTHIANS 4:14 (NEB)

When [my friend] arrived in the morning it was to be told that quietly and peacefully during the night his beloved mother had gone across to the other side. There she lay peacefully. He looked upon her face, upon the lips that would not speak again and remembered that the last words he had heard her say he would never forget: *"I'll see you in the morning."* . . . I asked him what he thought about that. . . . He looked at me with a face full of surprise. "Why, of course," he said, "I'll see her in the morning. . . . Don't you remember . . . the dear old hymn, 'There's a land that is fairer than day and by faith we can see it afar.' And the refrain, 'In the sweet by-and-by we shall meet on that beautiful shore.' Oh, yes," he said, "I haven't the slightest doubt at all that I will see her in the morning."

Norman Vincent Peale

There's a land that is fairer than day,
And by faith we can see it afar;
For the Father waits over the way,
To prepare us a dwelling-place there.

We shall sing on that beautiful shore
The melodious songs of the blest.
And our spirits shall sorrow no more
Not a sigh for the blessing of rest.

To our bountiful Father above,
We will offer our tribute of praise,
For the glorious gift of His love,
And the blessings that hallow our days.

In the sweet by and by,
We shall meet on that beautiful shore;
In the sweet by and by,
We shall meet on that beautiful shore.

S. Filmore Bennett

(Ed note: the mistakes in spelling are as in the original letter)

My Dear Daughter . . . I know of nothing on this earth that would gratify me so much as to meet with My Dear & only daughter, I fear that I should not be able to retain my senses on account of the great Joy it would creat in me, But time alone will develup whether this meeting will tak place on earth or not Hope keeps the soul alive, but my Dear Daughter if this should not be our happy lot, I pray God that we may be able to hold fast to the end, & be the Happy recipients of the promise made to the faithful. There will be no parting there but we shall live in the immediate presence and smiles of our God . . . May God guide and protect you through Life, & Finally save You in Heaven is the prayer of your affectionate mother.

Letter from a slave mother to her free daughter

Those who live in the Lord never see each other for the last time.

German motto

Many of the slave songs and spirituals were plaintive cries to God for help and understanding. . . . The pain and anguish of the present—especially the heartbreak of family separation—was alleviated only by the powerful hope of reuniting again in the life hereafter:

Ruth A. Tucker

When we all meet in Heaven
There is no parting there;
When we all meet in Heaven,
There is no more parting there.
See wives and husbands sold apart,
Their children's screams will break my heart—
There's a better day a coming,
Will you go along with me?
There's a better day a coming,
God sound the jubilee.

Finish then Thy new creation,
  Pure and spotless let us be;
Let us see Thy great salvation,
  Perfectly restored in Thee;
Changed from Glory into glory,
Till in heaven we take our place,
Till we cast our crowns before Thee,
  Lost in wonder, love, and praise!

Charles Wesley

Lord I want to die
in my sleep
I want to go to bed
and be awakened
by you
saying
Get up son
it's the first day of school
the beginning of your new job
the dawn of eternity.
Here are your clothes.
Your older brother
wore them first
now they're yours
forever
white and fresh and clean
smelling of heaven.

Joseph Bayly

Serving God in heaven is work as free from care and toil and fatigue as is the wing-stroke of the jubilant lark when it soars into the sunlight of a fresh, clear day and, spontaneously and for self-relief, pours out its thrilling carol. Work up there is a matter of self-relief, as well as a matter of obedience to the ruling of God. It is work according to one's tastes and delight and ability. If tastes vary there, if abilities vary there, then occupations will vary there.

David Gregg

Donald Grey Barnhouse used to speculate in his Monday night New York Bible Class. What would heaven be like? He didn't know, of course. But he was quite sure that God had wonders beyond description in mind.

"I expect that one day God will tell me, 'Donald, go create a world and people it and govern it for Me,'" Barnhouse would say. Somehow he felt that the whole re-created universe, with its myriads of galaxies and uncounted stars, should be filled with beings who loved and worshiped God, and found great joy in Him. To Barnhouse this earth, and our race, was but a seed. And when that seed sprouted, and history had run its course, a redeemed humanity would be the agency through which God spread the knowledge of Himself through an endless multitude of possible worlds.

Larry Richards

This love of Christ, if I may so say, will keep the saints in an employ, even when they are in heaven; though not an employ that is laborsome, tiresome, burdensome, yet an employ that is dutiful, delightful, and profitable; for although the work and worship of saints in heaven is not particularly revealed as yet, and so it doth not yet appear what we shall be, yet in the general we may say, there will be that for them to do that has not yet by them been done; and by that work which they shall do there, their delight will be unto them.

John Bunyan

I sat with a friend recently in his hospital room. The diagnosis is terminal cancer. If death comes, it will interrupt a distinguished career as a leader in training young men to serve Jesus Christ.

"When we think of heaven," he said, "I don't think we give enough consideration to what we're told in Revelation, that 'His servants serve Him,' and that their service is 'day and night.' We talk too much about rest—our rest will be found in serving God."

Joseph Bayly

In mansions of glory and endless delight,
I'll ever adore Thee in heaven so bright;
I'll sing with the glittering crown on my brow;
If ever I loved Thee, my Jesus, 'tis now.

William R. Featherstone

I stand on the shores of eternity and cry out, "Eternity! Eternity! How long art thou?" Back comes the answer, "How long? When ten thousand times ten thousand times ten thousand years have passed, eternity will have just begun."

Billy Sunday

And when this flesh and heart shall fail,
And mortal life shall cease;
I shall possess within the veil
A life of joy and peace.

When we've been there ten thousand years,
Bright shining as the sun,
We've no less days to sing God's praise
Than when we first begun.

John Newton

Our risen heart, sin-free will be
pure passion poured
purely
Adore!
He will give us this heart free
to love for the first time again.
Our risen body, light, bright
clothed in righ-
teousness, blessed with glowing flesh
that feels, really feels for the first time again.
But now we wait
wait
wait for our Risen Lord
who will reward we who weep
yet still seek Him above all
so . . .
stand we tall together
for the first time ever
then fall, please, on grateful knees. . . .
Eternity is ours.

Joni Eareckson Tada

To give this body, racked
With mortal ills and cares,
For one as glorious and as fair,
As our Redeemer wears;

To run, to leap, to walk,
To quit our beds of pain,
And live where the inhabitants
Are never sick again;

Thank God! for all my loved,
That out of pain and care,
Have safely reached the heavenly heights,
And stay to meet me there!

Phoebe Cary

It was the light, the grass, the trees that were different; made of some different substance, so much solider than things in our country . . . I saw people coming to meet us. Because they were bright I saw them while they were still very distant . . . the earth shook under their tread as their strong feet sank into the wet turf. A tiny haze and a sweet smell went up where they had crushed the grass and scattered the dew . . . the robes did not disguise the massive grandeur of muscle and the radiant smoothness of flesh . . . no one struck me as being of any particular age. One gets glimpses even in our country of that which is ageless—heavy thought in the face of an infant, and frolic childhood in that of a very old man. Here it was all like that.

C.S. Lewis

Heaven

A place with no room for sorrow
and suffering.

*"And I heard a loud voice from the throne saying,
'Now the dwelling of God is with men, and he will live
with them. They will be his people, and God himself will
be with them and be their God. He will wipe every tear
from their eyes. There will be no more death or mourning
or crying or pain, for the old order of things has
passed away.'"*

REVELATION 21:3-4

Be still, my soul: the hour is hastening on
When we shall be forever with the Lord,
When disappointment, grief, and fear are gone,
Sorrow forgot, love's purest joys restored.
Be still, my soul: when change and tears are past,
All safe and blessed we shall meet at last.

Katharina von Schlegel

One day the dream will come true.

One day, if I should die before Jesus returns, my soul will be reunited with my body. Pause and dream with me. . .

One day no more bulging middles or balding tops. No varicose veins or crow's-feet. No more cellulite or support hose. Forget the thunder thighs and highway hips. Just a quick leapfrog over the tombstone and it's the body you've always dreamed of. Fit and trim, smooth and sleek.

It makes me want to break up into giggles right now! Little wonder "we eagerly await a Savior from [heaven], the Lord Jesus Christ, who, by the power that enables him to bring everything under his control, will transform our lowly bodies so that they will be like his glorious body" (Philippians 3:20-21).

Joni Eareckson Tada

All too many of us know what it is to have our future stolen. The things we've planned and looked forward to can be taken by a loved one's death. By a lost job. By an illness. By war, fire, or theft. There are no guarantees given to any of us for what tomorrow may hold.

But still, no one can really steal our future. . . Beyond tomorrow you and I have treasures that no one can touch. In the words of Isaiah, we look forward to a time when "the Lord will be your ever-lasting light, and your God will be your glory. Your sun will never set again, and your moon will wane no more; the Lord will be your everlasting light, and your days of sorrow will end."

How good to remember when someone or some event steals tomorrow, that beyond tomorrow, our eternal future remains secure.

Larry Richards

Suffering hurries the heart homeward.

Joni Eareckson Tada

What is heaven like?

For the tired, it is a place of rest. For the sorrowing, a place where "God shall wipe away all tears from their eyes; and there shall be no more death, neither sorrow, nor crying" . . . or war or greed or evil of any kind.

For all it is a place of total happiness: "In thy presence is fulness of joy; at thy right hand there are pleasures for evermore" (Psalm 16:11, KJV).

Joseph Bayly

Trying to understand what our bodies will be like in heaven is much like expecting an acorn to understand his destiny of roots, bark, branches, and leaves. Or asking a caterpillar to appreciate flying. Or a peach pit to fathom being fragrant. Or a coconut to grasp what it means to sway in the ocean breeze. Our eternal bodies will be so grand, so glorious, that we can only catch a fleeting glimpse of the splendor to come. C.S. Lewis marveled: "It is a serious thing to live in a society of possible gods and goddesses."

Joni Eareckson Tada

One day everything on earth will perish and disappear, because the whole earth is defiled and corrupted. By great and marvelous contrast, however, one day every believer will "obtain an inheritance which is imperishable and undefiled and will not fade away" (1 Peter 1:4). It is that very inheritance that is "reserved in heaven" for us. What a wonderful prize awaits us when we cross the finish line in pursuit of our glorious Lord and Savior.

John MacArthur, Jr.

Not now, but in the coming years,
It may be in the better land,
We'll read the meaning of our tears,
And there, some time, we'll understand.

We'll catch the broken thread again,
And finish what we here began;
Heav'n will the mysteries explain,
And then, ah, then, we'll understand.

We'll know why clouds instead of sun
Were over many a cherished plan;
Why song has ceased when scarce begun;
'Tis there, some time, we'll understand.

Why what we long for most of all,
Elludes so oft our eager hand;
Why hopes are crushed and castles fall,
Up there, some time, we'll understand.

God knows the way, He holds the key,
He guides us with unerring hand;
Some time with tearless eyes we'll see;
Yes, there, up there, we'll understand.

Maxwell N. Cornelius

There is another song we need to sing at Christmastime. Not "Joy to the World," not "O Little Town of Bethlehem," but "Were You There When They Crucified My Lord?"

Were you there?

Not as an observer, but as a participant. Not as a scoffer, but as one who was so perfectly united with our Lord through faith that His death was yours, His blood payment for your sins, His suffering your passport to eternal joy.

If you were there, at Calvary, you can be sure that one day you will stand with the white-robed throng before God's throne, and know the joy of the redeemed.

Never again to hunger.

Never again to thirst.

Never again to weep a tear.

For then the Lamb, at the center of God's throne, will be your Shepherd and your joy.

Larry Richards

Maybe you can remember saying in your heart, Oh this day is so good—I wish it could last forever! That's what Heaven is. It's a good day that lasts forever.

The golden light will never fade into dark. The little flowers in the meadow will never die or wither. The fresh, excited feeling you have when you bound out of bed in the morning will never wear off. The joy will never turn into disappointment. The fun will never change into something you feel sorry about. The laughter and happiness will never be spoiled by having to leave or quit or say goodbye.

Larry Libby

Can you imagine the disciples' excitement as they heard about heaven? "Sounds beautiful. I can't wait to see it!" "I'll be glad to be free from the constant pain in my knee." "Never again will I have to bury someone I love."

In heaven you will *never* hear:
"Your mortgage is due."
"Sorry. We can't use you."
"Stop worrying."
"The doctor says it's hopeless."
"Your child has just been in an accident."
"What you are asking is impossible."

You *will* hear:
"Holy, holy, holy is the Lord God Almighty."
"Wow!"
"How wonderful to see you again."
"It sure feels good to be home."

Lorraine Pintus

HEAVEN

A place where death has been defeated
and resurrection is reality.

"Jesus said to her, 'I am the resurrection and the life.
He who believes in me will live, even though he dies, and
whoever lives and believes in me wil never die."

JOHN 11:25-26

The world recedes; it disappears!
Heaven opens on my eyes! my ears
With sounds seraphic ring!
Lend, lend your wings! I mount! I fly!
O Grave! where is thy victory?
O Death! where is thy sting?

Alexander Pope

In our cold times, we have a "seed catalog." We open it and smell the promised spring, eternal spring. And the firstfruit that settles our hope is Jesus Christ, who was raised from death and cold earth to glory eternal.

Joseph Bayly

What blessed assurance for Christians of all ages. Christ is alive. And He has the keys to the gates of death and hell.

Has the gate of death opened to admit your beloved—parent, child, loved one, friend? Jesus was there with the keys of death. He has the key to every grave in every quiet country graveyard and crowded city cemetery. He is the custodian of the treasure beneath that mound of earth, decked with fragrant flowers. His own mighty resurrection and power are the keys that unlock that gate and bid the imprisoned body arise to newness of life in likeness of His own. He is the Living One and because He lives, we shall live also.

Henry Gariepy

One of the great souls of our time, Episcopal Bishop Warren Chandler, lay dying. An old friend sitting by his bedside asked him about his feelings. "Please tell me frankly, do you dread crossing the river of death?" "Why," Bishop Chandler replied, "My Father owns the land on both sides of the river. Why should I be afraid?"

Bruce Larson

I cannot prove the existence of heaven.

I accept its reality by faith, on the authority of Jesus Christ.

For that matter, if I were a twin in the womb, I doubt that I could prove the existence of earth to my mate. He would probably object that the idea of an earth beyond the womb was ridiculous, that the womb was the only earth we'd ever know.

If I tried to explain that earthlings live in a greatly expanded environment and breathe air, he would only be more skeptical. After all, a fetus lives in water; who could imagine its being able to live in a universe of air? To him such a transition would seem impossible.

It would take birth to prove the earth's existence to a fetus. A little pain, a dark tunnel, a gasp of air—and then the wide world!

Joseph Bayly

"Where is Sonny Boy? Where is he?" . . . And I answer it now: "He is with the Lord."

But I want to refine that answer until it truly comforts you, Gloria. It is not meant cheaply. It comes after long thought.

Listen: when Sonny Boy left this life, he left creation as God gave it unto us. He left all things and the space that contains things. He left history and the time that contains history. He departed *time*, Gloria, immediately and entirely to be with God.

You and I are still inside of time. We still move in tiny ticks of seconds through long months and the interminable years. Through days and days we creep toward the Last Day, when all of us will meet God, the living and the dead together, because on that Day the dead will be raised to life, and Sonny Boy too.

From our perspective, that's a long *time* away.

But Sonny Boy has popped free of time. From *his* perspective, there is no time any more. He doesn't have to wait. He is there already! For him it is already the Great Gettin'-Up Morning—and he's up!

Walter Wangerin, Jr.

Christ has made of death a narrow, starlit strip between the companionships of yesterday and the reunions of tomorrow.

William Jennings Bryan

If the Father deigns to touch with divine power the cold and pulseless heart of the buried acorn and to make it burst forth from its prison walls, will He leave neglected in the earth the soul of man made in the image of his Creator?

William Jennings Bryan

The glorious fact that the empty tomb proclaims to us is that life for us does not stop when death comes.

Death is not a wall, but a door.

And eternal life which may be ours now, by faith in Christ, is not interrupted when the soul leaves the body, for we live on . . . and on.

There is no death to those who have entered into fellowship with Him who emerged from the tomb.

Peter Marshall

The hope that Christians will overcome the grave and spend eternity with God is not the desperate longing of people too afraid to face their own mortality. Instead, it's a rational and logical conclusion based on the compelling testimony of history.

"No intelligent jury in the world," said Lord Darling, the brilliant chief justice of England, "could fail to bring in a verdict that the Resurrection story is true."

Lee Strobel

Death be not proud
though some have called thee
mighty and dreadful
for thou art not so.
For those whom thou thinkest
thou dost overthrow
die not, poor death.
nor yet canst thou kill me . . .
One short sleep past
we wake eternally
and death shall be no more.
Death, thou shalt die.

John Donne

A friend of mine was forced to leave inland China with his wife and small children when the Communists took over the country in 1949. Each night of their flight to the coast they slept in a different peasant hut.

One night his wife died quite suddenly and unexpectedly. When morning came, he had to explain to his children that their mother had died, and also—seemingly most difficult for children to understand—that they would have to leave their mother's body behind, buried in the ground, and continue their flight.

"If ever I prayed for wisdom, for the right words, it was then. And God gave them to me. I reminded the children that we had stayed in different huts, and when morning came, we went on, leaving the hut behind.

"Mother's body was the house in which she lived, I explained. During the night, God told her to come home. So she went, leaving behind the house in which she'd been staying. That house was her body, and we loved it, but Mother no longer lived in it. So we would leave it there and put it in the ground when we left in a few hours. Somehow they accepted that simple explanation."

The simple explanation was also the true one. . . My friend could have added, and doubtless later did, that God loves Mother's body, too—not just her spirit—and someday will perform the miracle of resurrection. Then He will make her body more alive than it ever was and reunite it with Mother's spirit—just as He did for our Lord Jesus on Easter morning.

Joseph Bayly

On December 7, 1941, Peter Marshall, the famed chaplain of the U.S. Senate, was speaking to the cadets at Annapolis, unaware that as he spoke Pearl Harbor was in flames. Many in his audience would be called upon to give their lives in the days ahead. He told them this story.

"A young boy dying from an incurable disease asked his mother, 'What is it like to die? Does it hurt?'

"His mother answered: 'Remember when you were a very little boy and played very hard and fell asleep on mommy's bed? When you woke in the morning you were in your own bed because your daddy came with his big strong arms and lifted you, undressed you, and put on your pajamas. Death is like that—you wake up in your own room.'"

Jeanne Hendricks

Christ the Lord is risen today, Alleluia!
Sons of men and angels say, Alleluia!
Raise your joys and triumphs high, Alleluia!
Sing, ye heavens, and earth, reply, Alleluia!

Love's redeeming work is done, Alleluia!
Fought the fight, the battle won, Alleluia!
Death in vain forbids Him rise, Alleluia!
Christ hath opened paradise, Alleluia!

Soar we now where Christ has led, Alleluia!
Following our exalted Head, Alleluia!
Made like Him, like Him we rise, Alleluia!
Ours the cross, the grave, the skies, Alleluia!

Charles Wesley

HEAVEN

With confidence and thanksgiving,
we look forward to a place
called Heaven.

*"But in keeping with his promise we are
looking forward to a new heaven and a new earth,
the home of righteousness."*

2 PETER 3:13

I thank Thee, O Lord, that Thou hast so set eternity within my heart that no earthly thing can ever satisfy me wholly.

John Baillie

Oh, I wish He would come today, so that I could lay my crowns at His feet!

Queen Victoria

Those who live by faith, walk by faith . . . They do not dwell but only sojourn here; not looking upon earth as their home, but only "Travelling through Immanuel's ground, To fairer worlds on high."

John Wesley

The problem with this world is that it doesn't fit. Oh, it will do for now, but it isn't tailor-made. We were made to live with God, but on earth we live by faith. We were made to live forever, but on this earth we live but for a moment. We were made to live holy lives, but this world is stained by sin. This world wears like a borrowed shirt. Heaven, however, will fit like one tailor-made.

Max Lucado

On Earth, you will always feel a bit restless. This is not your home. *Heaven* is your home. Ponder its existence. Long for it. "Set your mind on things above, not on earthly things." Remember, "our citizenship is in heaven. And we eagerly await a Savior from there, the Lord Jesus Christ."

Lorraine Pintus

The Bible provides the symbols. But it is faith that makes the hieroglyphics of heaven come alive. And heaven *has* to come alive! After all, you're a citizen of the kingdom of heaven and according to Philippians 3:20, you're supposed to be eagerly awaiting it. Heaven is your journey's end, your life's goal, your purpose for going on. If heaven is the home of your spirit, the rest for your soul, the repository of every spiritual investment on earth, then it must grip your heart. And your heart must grip heaven by faith.

Joni Eareckson Tada

There have been times when I think we do not desire heaven but more often I find myself wondering whether, in our heart of hearts, we have ever desired anything else.

C.S. Lewis

Every day of our lives we are just a breath away from eternity. The believer in Jesus Christ has the promises of heaven. If we believe them, the anticipation of heaven will never be boring. It will be more thrilling than any of the pleasures earth can offer.

Billy Graham

So it's beyond what the Bible says.

"Far, far beyond. How could
a twin born into earthworld describe
what he saw, just in the
delivery room even, to his twin not
yet born? And beyond the
delivery room would be the
Rocky Mountains,
the sky on a starry night,
animals on an African game farm."

Maybe that's why Isaiah's vision and
Daniel's descriptions of the
great beasts always
seemed so strange
to me, and a lot of things in
Revelation. I never could get a clear
sight on what angels looked like.
"You'll soon see them. And they won't
seem strange any longer,
just beautiful and full of power, like
all that I create."

Joseph Bayly

O Lord,
I live here as a fish in a vessel of water,
only enough to keep me alive,
but in heaven I shall swim in the ocean.
Here I have a little air in me to keep me breathing,
but there I shall have sweet and fresh gales;
Here I have a beam of sun to lighten my darkness,
a warm ray to keep me from freezing;
yonder I shall live in light and warmth forever.

A Puritan prayer

O weary soul, still follow Him,
The night will soon be gone;
Rest waits beyond the shadows dim,
A little farther on.

O burdened soul, trust on, be true,
Tho' strength seems nearly gone;
The gates of home will be in view
A little farther on.

O longing heart, tho' from thy side
Thy friends have long been gone,
Each longing will be satisfied
A little farther on!

James Rowe

This world is not my home, I'm just a passing through,
My treasures are laid up somewhere beyond the blue;
The angels beckon me from heaven's open door,
And I can't feel at home in this world anymore.

A.E. Brumley

A continual looking forward to the eternal world is
not a form of escapism or wishful thinking, but one
of the things a Christian is meant to do. It does not
mean that we are to leave the present world as it is.
If you read history, you will find that the Christians
who did the most for the present world were just
those who thought most of the next.

C.S. Lewis

... life defines in the autumn
the gathering spirit ripens
in the seasoned flesh of the years
the bones appear
the face weathers
the fruit is borne

there comes a comfortable chill
to the night air
and harvest
draws
near

Robert A. Raines

Swing low, sweet chariot,
Comin' for to carry me home,
Swing low, sweet chariot,
Comin' for to carry me home.

I look'd over Jordan,
An' what did I see,
Comin' for to carry me home?
A band of angels comin' after me,
Comin' for to carry me home.

If you get-a dere befo' I do,
Comin' for to carry me home,
Tell all my friends I'm comin' too,
Comin' for to carry me home.

Negro Spiritual

And when my task on earth is done,
When, by thy grace, the victory's won,
E'en death's cold wave I will not flee,
Since God through Jordan leadeth me.

Joseph H. Gilmore

How far away is heaven? It is not so far as some imagine. It wasn't very far from Daniel. It was not so far off that Elijah's prayer, and those of others could not be heard there. Christ said when ye pray say, "Our father, who art in heaven." Men full of the Spirit can look right into heaven.

Dwight L. Moody

I never saw a Moor—
I never saw the Sea—
Yet know I how the Heather looks
And what a wave must be.

I never spoke with God
Nor visited in Heaven—
Yet certain am I of the spot
As if the chart were given—

Emily Dickinson

One sweetly solemn thought
Comes to me o'er and o'er;
Nearer my home today am I
Than e'er I've been before.

Nearer my Father's house,
Where many mansions be;
Nearer today, the great white throne,
Nearer the crystal sea.

Nearer the bound of life,
Where burdens are laid down,
Nearer to leave the heavy cross,
Nearer to gain the crown.

Phoebe Cary

I shall know why—when Time is over—
And I have ceased to wonder why—
Christ will explain each separate anguish
In the fair schoolroom of the sky—

He will tell me what "Peter" promised—
And I—for wonder at his woe—
I shall forget the drop of Anguish
That scalds me now—that scalds me now!

Emily Dickinson

O that with yonder sacred throng
We at His feet may fall!
We'll join the everlasting song,
And crown Him Lord of all!

Edward Perronet

This day, I saw clearly that I should never be happy, yea, that God Himself could not make me happy, unless I could be in a capacity to "please and glorify Him forever." . . . Oh to love and praise God more, to please Him forever! This my soul panted after and even now pants for while I write. . . . And oh, I longed to be with God, to behold His glory and to bow in His presence!

David Brainerd

"I will dwell in the house of the Lord forever."
Psalm 23:6

The Lord is my shepherd; therefore, I shall not want forever. Eternity is a rather long time. Most of our minds are incapable of even starting to comprehend what it means.

I don't think about eternity a lot. But when I do, I'm grateful to know that it's in His hands, and not mine, and that I shall not be found wanting. Eternal life began when the first connection and commitment was made to Jesus Christ. According to the rumor, it has no end. I rather like that.

Tim Hansel

Unnumber'd years of bliss
I to my sheep will give;
And while my throne unshaken stands
Shall all my chosen live.

Enough, my gracious Lord,
Let faith triumphant cry;
My heart can on this promise live,
Can with this promise die.

Abraham Lincoln

A little girl was walking with her father in the country. No neon sign, no automobile headlights or street lamps marred the stillness of the crisp evening. As she looked into the deep blue velvet sky, studded with an array of diamonds which put the most dazzling Tiffany display to shame, she said, "Daddy, if the wrong side of heaven is so beautiful, what do you think the right side will be like?"

Some day all believers in Jesus Christ will see the "right side" of heaven.

Billy Graham

Bring us, O Lord God, at the last awakening into the house and gate of heaven, to enter into that gate and dwell in that house, where there shall be no darkness nor dazzling, but one equal light; no noise nor silence, but one equal music; no fears nor hopes, but an equal possession; no ends nor beginnings, but one equal eternity, in the habitations of thy majesty and thy glory, world without end.

John Donne

"That is what is meant by the Scriptures which say that no mere man has ever seen, heard or even imagined what wonderful things God has ready for those who love the Lord."

1 Corinthians 2:9 (TLB)

ACKNOWLEDGMENTS

Reasonable care has been taken to trace ownership of the materials quoted from in this book, and to obtain permission to use copyrighted materials, when necessary.

A Farthing Oak—Meditations From the Mountain, Robert Raines, 1982, Crossroad Publishing Co., New York, New York. All rights reserved.

Facing Death and Life After, Billy Graham, 1987, Word, Inc., Dallas, Texas. All rights reserved.

Heaven—Your Real Home by Joni Eareckson Tada. Copyright © 1995 by Joni Eareckson Tada. Used by permission of Zondervan Publishing House.

Living Beyond Our Fears, Bruce Larson, 1990, Harper San Francisco, San Francisco, California. All rights reserved.

Mourning Into Dancing by Walter Wangerin, Jr.. Copyright © 1992 by Walter Wangerin, Jr.. Used by permission of Zondervan Publishing House.